I0606288

Best Inventions

Aircraft

by Julie Murray

Dash!
LEVELED READERS
An Imprint of Abdo Zoom • abdobooks.com

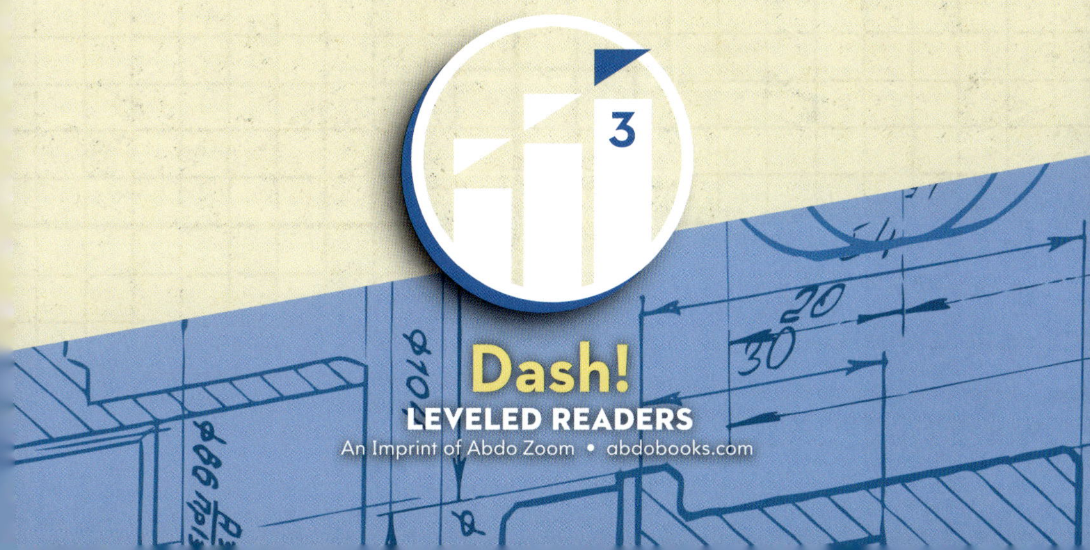

Level 1 – Beginning
Short and simple sentences with familiar words or patterns for children who are beginning to understand how letters and sounds go together.

Level 2 – Emerging
Longer words and sentences with more complex language patterns for readers who are practicing common words and letter sounds.

Level 3 – Transitional
More developed language and vocabulary for readers who are becoming more independent.

abdobooks.com

Published by Abdo Zoom, a division of ABDO, PO Box 398166, Minneapolis, Minnesota 55439.

Printed in the United States of America, North Mankato, Minnesota.
102022
012023

Photo Credits: Alamy, Getty Images, Shutterstock
Production Contributors: Kenny Abdo, Jennie Forsberg, Grace Hansen, John Hansen
Design Contributors: Candice Keimig, Neil Klinepier, Colleen McLaren

Library of Congress Control Number: 2022937320

Publisher's Cataloging in Publication Data

Names: Murray, Julie, author.
Title: Aircraft / by Julie Murray
Description: Minneapolis, Minnesota : Abdo Zoom, 2023 | Series: Best inventions | Includes online resources and index.
Identifiers: ISBN 9781098280154 (lib. bdg.) | ISBN 9781098280680 (ebook) | ISBN 9781098280987 (Read-to-Me ebook)
Subjects: LCSH: Airplanes--Juvenile literature. | Inventions--Juvenile literature. | Aeronautics--Juvenile literature. | Inventions--History--Juvenile literature.
Classification: DDC 629.133--dc23

Table of Contents

Aircraft

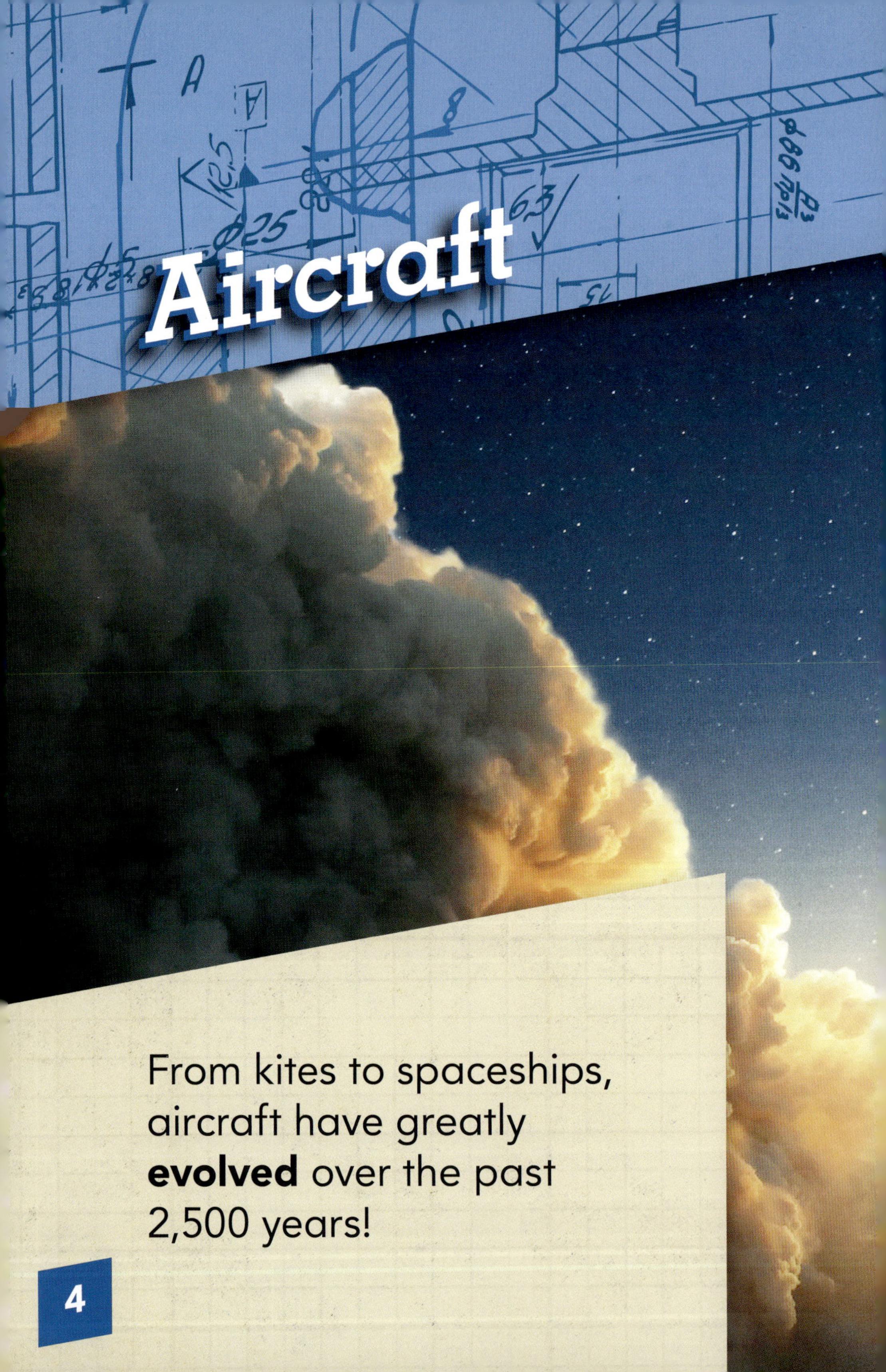

From kites to spaceships, aircraft have greatly **evolved** over the past 2,500 years!

20
30
130
45

History

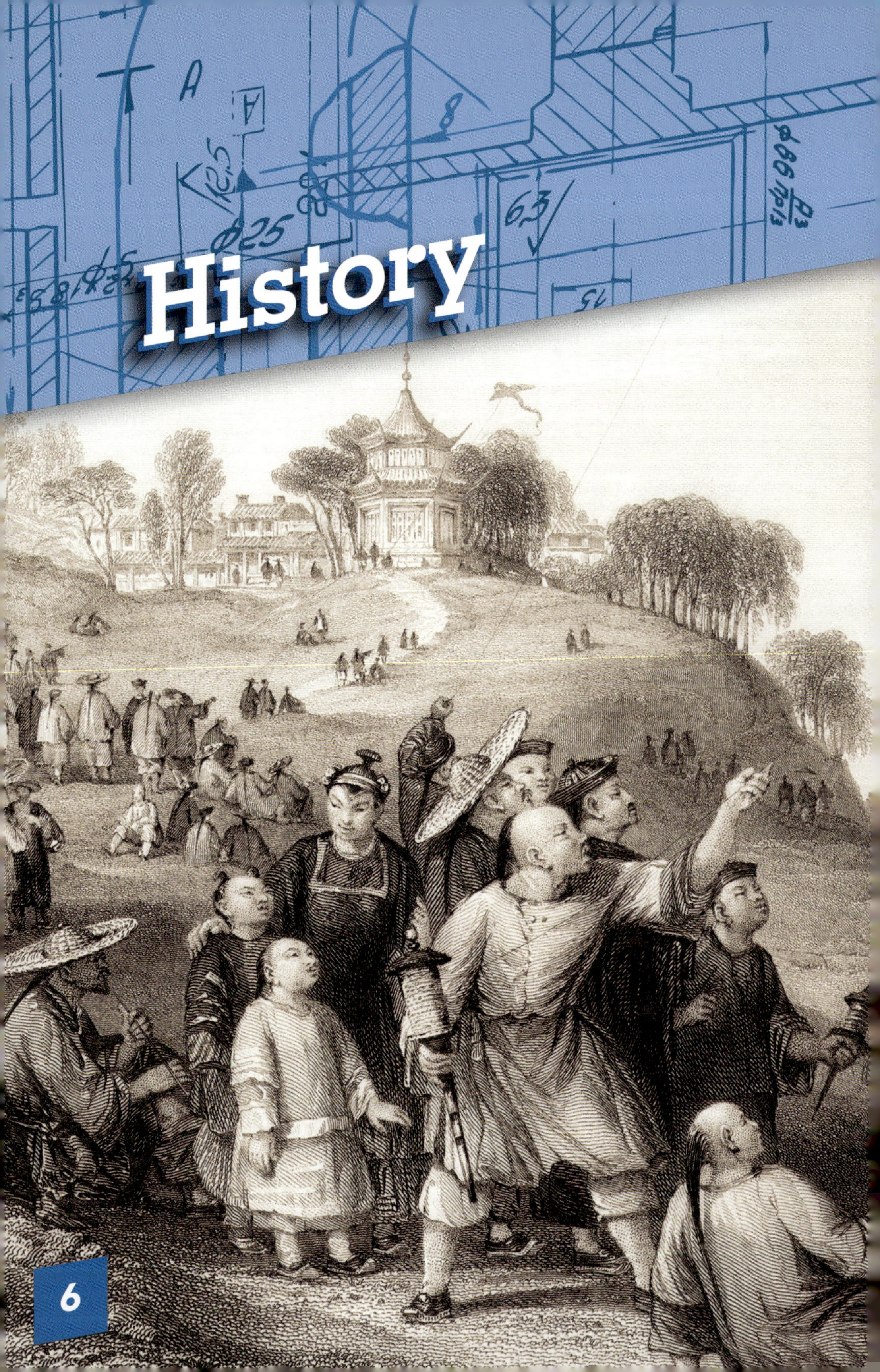

An aircraft is any machine that can fly. Kites were the first aircraft. They were used in China as early as 200 BCE. Kites had many uses throughout history.

The first manned flight of an aircraft took place in France in 1783. Étienne Montgolfier left the ground in the hot air balloon he and his brother invented.

The Wright brothers made aircraft history on December 17, 1903. They had the first successful flight of a motor-operated airplane at Kitty Hawk, North Carolina.

Types of Aircraft

A glider is an aircraft with no **engine**. It must be pulled or towed into the air. Once in the air, the glider flies using the rising air around it.

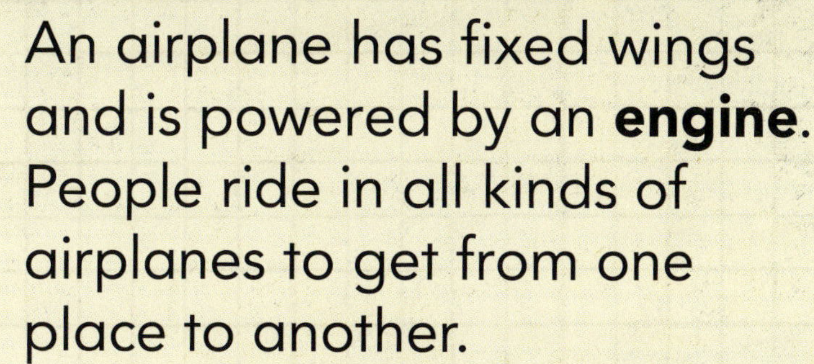

An airplane has fixed wings and is powered by an **engine**. People ride in all kinds of airplanes to get from one place to another.

Helicopters have **rotor blades** that spin. The main rotor blades above create lift. The tail rotor allows the aircraft to move in different directions.

rotor blade

Spacecraft can travel into space. **Propellants** give rocket **engines** enough energy to move the spacecraft away from Earth. Spacecraft can carry astronauts, **satellites**, and robots!

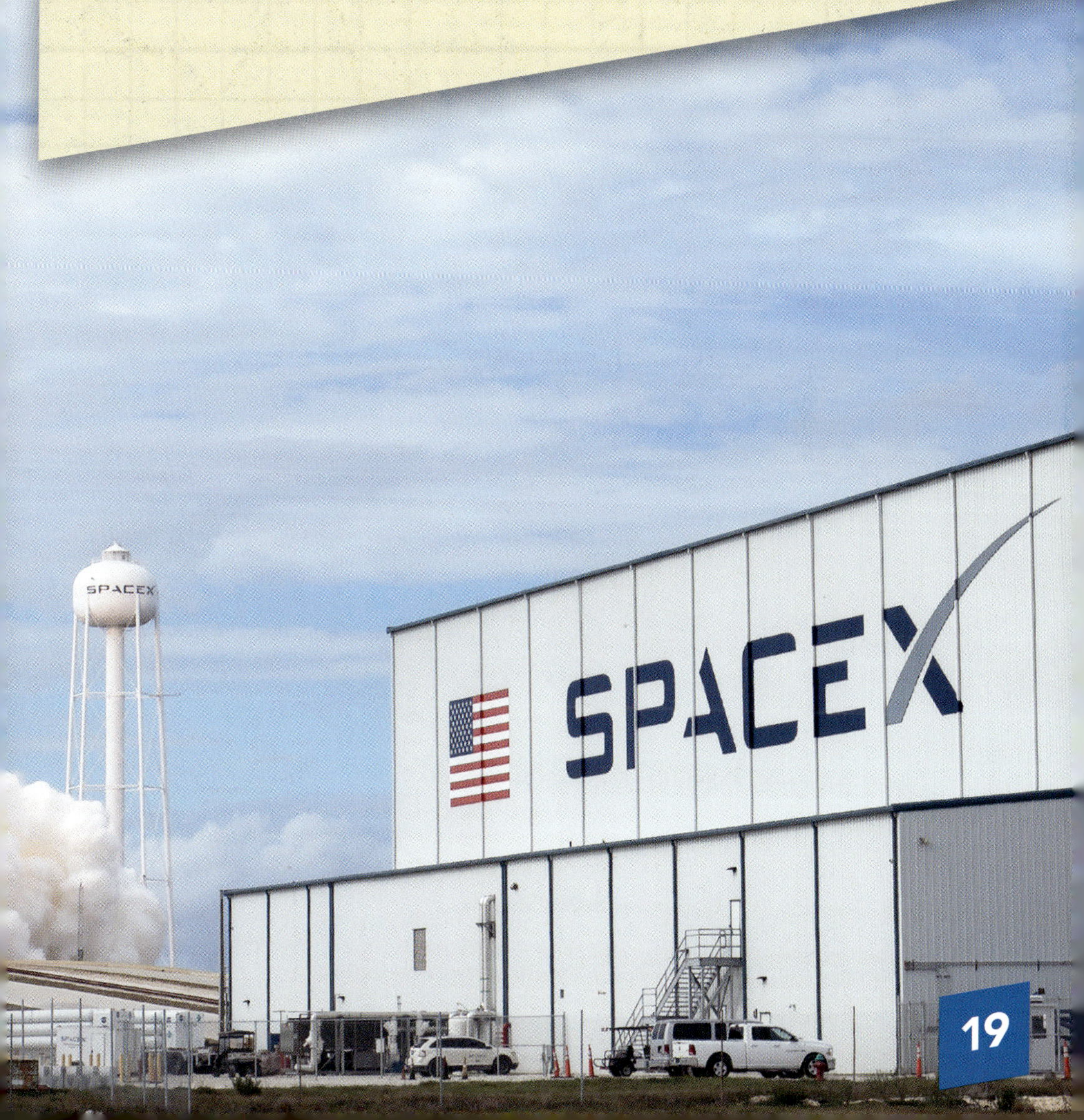

The invention of the aircraft has changed the world. Airplanes connect people around the globe. Spacecraft have allowed mankind to explore the **galaxy**.

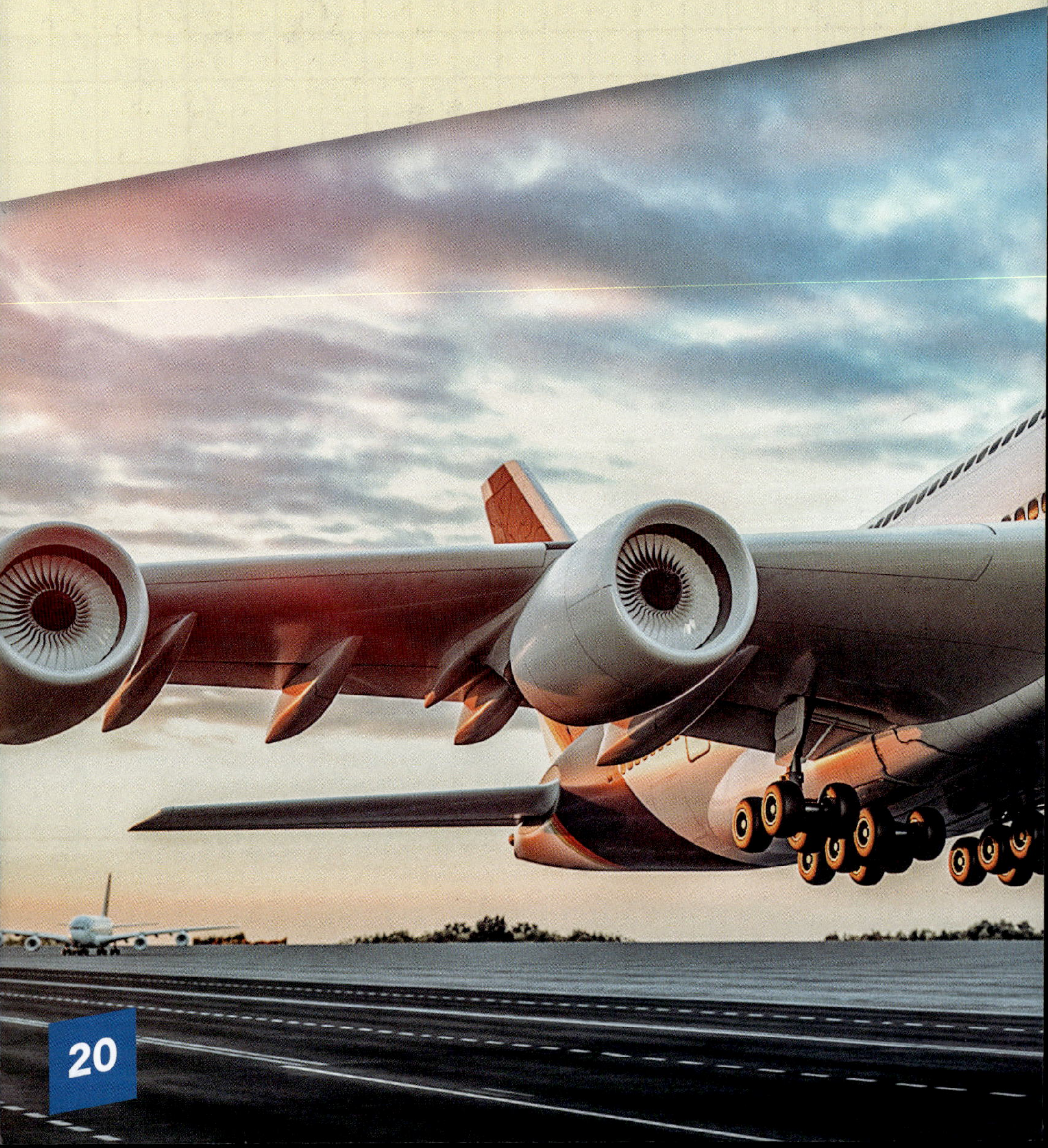

Who knows where aircraft will take people next!

More Facts

- Blimps are aircraft powered by light-weight gas. The most famous blimp was the *Hindenburg*. It was a passenger blimp. It exploded in 1937, killing 35 passengers.

- A biplane has two sets of wings. This was the type of aircraft the Wright brothers flew in 1903.

- More than 100,000 flights take off around the world each day.

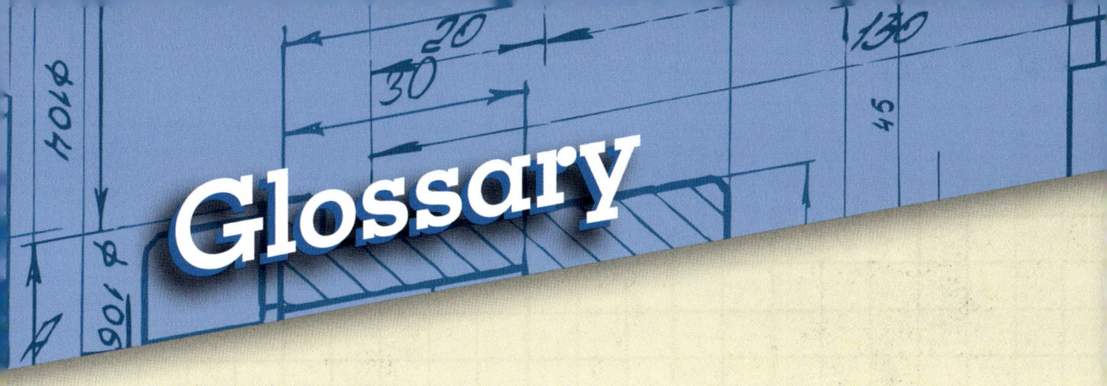

Glossary

engine – a machine that uses energy from fuel or electricity to do work, such as to move.

evolved – developed gradually or improved using steps.

galaxy – a collection of billions of stars and other matter held together by gravity. Our planet Earth and the sun belong to the Milky Way galaxy. They are only tiny parts of this galaxy.

propellant – fuel plus oxidizer used by a rocket engine.

rotor blade – one of the long blades that rotates to provide the lift that supports a helicopter in the air.

satellite – a spacecraft that is sent into orbit around a planet or other heavenly body to gather or send back information.

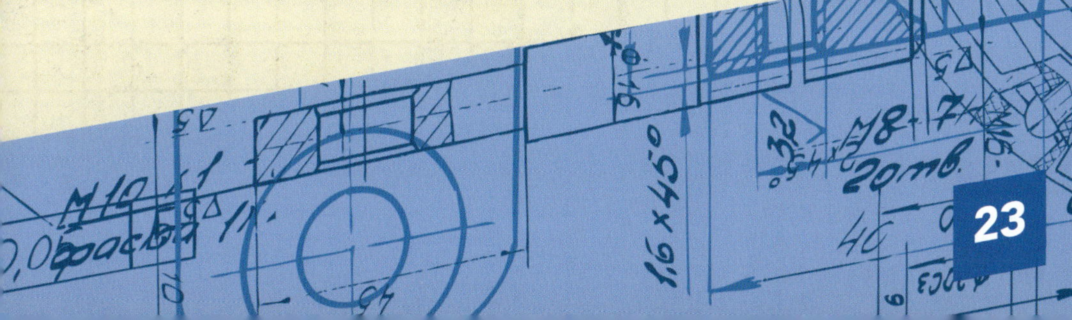

Index

Online Resources

To learn more about aircraft, please visit **abdobooklinks.com** or scan this QR code. These links are routinely monitored and updated to provide the most current information available.